Leo

por Patricia Abello

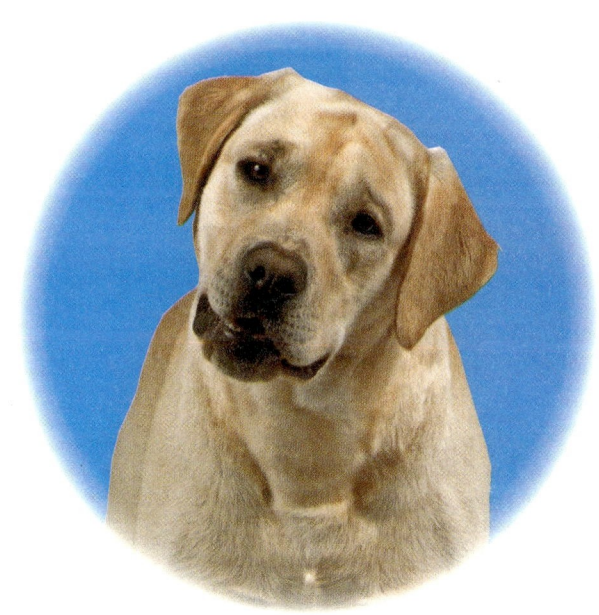

Scott Foresman
is an imprint of
PEARSON

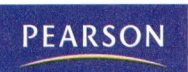

Glenview, Illinois • Boston, Massachusetts • Chandler, Arizona
Upper Saddle River, New Jersey

Every effort has been made to secure permission and provide appropriate credit for photographic material. The publisher deeply regrets any omission and pledges to correct errors called to its attention in subsequent editions.

Unless otherwise acknowledged, all photographs are the property of Pearson.

Photo locations denoted as follows: Top (T), Center (C), Bottom (B), Left (L), Right (R), Background (Bkgd)

Opener © Dorling Kindersley; 1 © Dorling Kindersley; 2 © Dorling Kindersley; 3 © Dorling Kindersley; 4 © Dorling Kindersley; 5 © Dorling Kindersley; 6 © Dorling Kindersley; 8 © Dorling Kindersley

ISBN 13: 978-0-328-53285-8
ISBN 10: 0-328-53285-1

Copyright © by Pearson Education, Inc., or its affiliates. All rights reserved. Printed in the United States of America. This publication is protected by copyright, and permission should be obtained from the publisher prior to any prohibited reproduction, storage in a retrieval system, or transmission in any form or by any means, electronic, mechanical, photocopying, recording, or likewise. For information regarding permissions, write to Pearson Curriculum Rights & Permissions, One Lake Street, Upper Saddle River, New Jersey 07458.

Pearson® is a trademark, in the U.S. and/or other countries, of Pearson plc or its affiliates.

Scott Foresman® is a trademark, in the U.S. and/or other countries, of Pearson Education, Inc., or its affiliates.

2 3 4 5 6 7 8 9 10 V0N4 13 12 11 10

Mira a Leo mi perro leal.

Leo no se siente bien.

Ella lo ayuda.

Leo no estaba feliz.

Ahora sí está feliz en su casa.

Medicinas para mascotas

Leamos juntos

Los veterinarios hacen medicinas especiales para mascotas. Hay medicinas para perros que saben a queso. Otras medicinas para gatos saben a pescado. Hay medicinas para pájaros que saben a fruta. ¿Qué sabor crees que tiene la medicina para conejos?